Lerner SPORTS™

I0866940

SUPER SPORTS TEAMS

INSIDE THE BROOKLYN NETS

LIZ SONNEBORN

Lerner Publications ◆ Minneapolis

Copyright © 2023 by Lerner Publishing Group, Inc.

All rights reserved. International copyright secured. No part of this book may be reproduced, stored in a retrieval system, or transmitted in any form or by any means—electronic, mechanical, photocopying, recording, or otherwise—without the prior written permission of Lerner Publishing Group, Inc., except for the inclusion of brief quotations in an acknowledged review.

Lerner Publications Company
An imprint of Lerner Publishing Group, Inc.
241 First Avenue North
Minneapolis, MN 55401 USA

For reading levels and more information, look up this title at www.lernerbooks.com.

Main body text set in Aptifer Slab LT Pro / Typeface provided by Linotype AG

Library of Congress Cataloging-in-Publication Data

Names: Sonneborn, Liz, author.
Title: Inside the Brooklyn Nets / Liz Sonneborn.
Description: Minneapolis, MN : Lerner Publications, 2023. | Series: Super sports teams. Lerner sports | Includes bibliographical references and index. | Audience: Ages 7–11 | Audience: Grades 4–6 | Summary: "The Brooklyn Nets boast some of basketball's best players, and they play exciting, high-energy games. Read about the team's history and highlights, and find out why Nets fans are excited for their team's future"— Provided by publisher.
Identifiers: LCCN 2022014236 (print) | LCCN 2022014237 (ebook) | ISBN 9781728476070 (library binding) | ISBN 9781728478654 (paperback) | ISBN 9781728485102 (ebook)
Subjects: LCSH: Brooklyn Nets (Basketball team)—History—Juvenile literature.
Classification: LCC GV885.52.B76 S66 2023 (print) | LCC GV885.52.B76 (ebook) | DDC 796.323/640974723—dc23/eng/20220328

LC record available at https://lccn.loc.gov/2022014236
LC ebook record available at https://lccn.loc.gov/2022014237

Manufactured in the United States of America
1 – CG – 12/15/22

TABLE OF CONTENTS

Kyrie Irving shoots a basket against the Bucks in 2021.

A FIGHT FOR THE FINALS

FACTS AT A GLANCE

- The Nets were formed in 1967 and got their start playing for New Jersey as the New Jersey Americans in the **AMERICAN BASKETBALL ASSOCIATION (ABA)**.
- Superstar **JULIUS ERVING** led the Nets to two ABA Championships.
- The Nets joined the **NATIONAL BASKETBALL ASSOCIATION (NBA)** in 1976.
- The **NETS** have never won an NBA title.

On June 19, 2021, the Brooklyn Nets entered their home court. They were ready to battle the Milwaukee Bucks in Game 7 of the Eastern Conference Semifinals. When the playoffs began, the Nets looked hard to beat. They had three superstar players—Kevin Durant, Kyrie Irving, and James Harden. Many fans thought the team would finally win their first NBA Championship.

The Nets took their first-round series against the Boston Celtics in five games. But just 43 seconds into Game 1 against the Bucks, the Nets were in trouble. Harden injured his leg. He was sidelined for the first four games of the series.

Then, Irving injured his ankle during Game 4. He was out for the rest of the series. All hopes for a win suddenly fell on Durant.

During Game 7, Durant never left the court. He scored 48 points, nearly matching his record-breaking 49 points in Game 5. His most amazing play happened in the game's final second. With the Nets down by two, he scored a 23-foot (7 m) jumper.

Durant was thrilled. He thought his three-pointer had won the series. But the replay showed his toes had been on the three-point line. Durant had scored only two points—tying, rather than winning, the game.

In overtime, the Bucks took a narrow lead. As the clock ticked down, Durant had another do-or-die moment. He took his final shot, hoping to force another overtime. This time, though, he came up short. The Bucks won 115–111, and the Nets were out of the playoffs.

Longtime Nets fans were disappointed but hardly surprised. They were used to the team's many ups and downs over their long history.

Durant takes control of a loose ball during the 2021 Eastern Conference Semifinals.

Durant averaged 35.4 points per game in the 2021 NBA Eastern Conference Semifinals.

Nets legend Julius "Dr. J" Erving (*second from the left*) is considered one of the greatest basketball players of all time.

ON THE MOVE

The Brooklyn Nets got their start playing as the New Jersey Americans. They were one of 11 teams formed in 1967 as part of the ABA.

The Americans were supposed to play in New York City. But the New York Knicks, an NBA team, objected. The Knicks did not want an ABA team playing in the same city as they did. The Americans were forced to move to New Jersey.

In their second season, the New Jersey Americans relocated to Long Island, New York. They also got a new name—the New York Nets. The Nets made it to the ABA Finals in 1972. But they only became champions after Julius Erving joined the team in 1973. He led the Nets to ABA titles in 1974 and 1976.

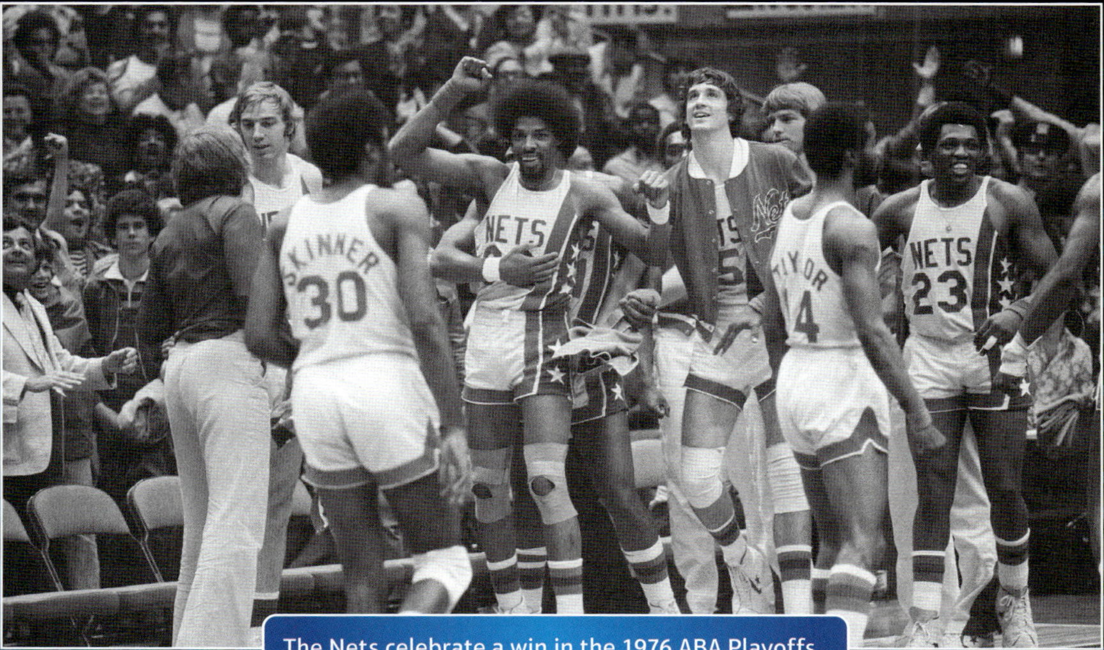

The Nets celebrate a win in the 1976 ABA Playoffs.

The Nets were doing great on the court. But the ABA was falling apart. Its teams were not making much money. Several went broke. Four of the remaining teams, including the Nets, decided to join the NBA in 1976.

For the Nets, the move came at a steep price. They had to pay the NBA and the Knicks millions of dollars. To make money, the Nets sold Erving's contract to the Philadelphia 76ers. Without their star player, the team struggled. During the Nets' first NBA season, they had a 22–60 record.

Jan van Breda Kolff played 434 games for the Nets from 1976 to 1983.

NETS FACT

The Nets' name was chosen because it rhymed with that of two other New York teams—the Jets (football) and the Mets (baseball).

The Nets played at the arena at Meadowlands Sports Complex from 1981 to 2010.

In 1977, the Nets returned to New Jersey. A few years later, they began playing at a new stadium in the Meadowlands Sports Complex. During the 1980s, they made the playoffs five years in a row (1982–1986). In the 1990s, they had a three-year streak (1992–1994), in addition to making the 1998 Playoffs. Yet, for most of these years, the Nets did not get past the opening round.

Kidd is ranked second in the NBA for career assists and steals.

The Nets had a comeback after trading for point guard Jason Kidd. They made it to the Finals in 2002 and 2003, but they lost both series. By the end of the decade, the team was struggling. Their 12–70 record in the 2009–2010 season was their worst ever.

In 2012, the Nets were again on the move. They relocated to Brooklyn, New York. The team played at a brand-new arena, the Barclays Center. There, the Brooklyn Nets began to rebuild their squad. They made it to the playoffs in 2013, 2014, and 2015.

In 2019, free agents Kevin Durant and Kyrie Irving signed with the team. The Nets had snagged two of the best players in the NBA. This new talent helped take the team to the playoffs in 2019, 2020, and 2021.

Irving dribbles down the court in a 2022 game.

Kenyon Martin helped the Nets reach the NBA Finals in 2002 and 2003.

AMAZING MOMENTS

The Nets have played plenty of exciting games. Some of the most thrilling happened when they were still an ABA team.

In their 1973–1974 season, the Nets won the ABA's Eastern Division with a 55–29 record. They soared through the playoffs, winning eight of their nine games. Game 1 of the Finals especially wowed fans. The Nets faced off against the Utah Stars. Nets superstar Julius Erving dominated the game. He scored an amazing 47 points, more than half of the Nets' total. The Nets took the title in just five games.

The Nets made the Finals again in 1976. Their rivals were the Denver Nuggets. Heading into Game 6, the Nets needed one more win for the championship.

Erving was known for his dunking skills.

The Nuggets came out strong. The Nets could not match their energy. In the second half, with only 17 minutes left, the Nets trailed by 22 points.

Nets guard "Super" John Williamson became determined to turn the game around. Williamson shot from all over the court, scoring jump shots, layups, and slam dunks. With just 2.19 minutes left, one of his jump shots gave the Nets the lead. The Nets pulled off a 112–106 win.

Martin averaged 16.8 points per game during the 2002 NBA Playoffs.

After the Nets joined the NBA, they did not make it to the league Finals for 26 years. They finally made it in 2002. They were up against the Los Angeles Lakers. Star players Shaquille O'Neal and Kobe Bryant had helped the Lakers win the championship the two previous years.

The Nets lost Game 1 by five points and Game 2 by 22 points. But they came roaring back in Game 3. Nets stars Jason Kidd, Kenyon Martin, and Richard Jefferson were playing better than ever.

NETS FACT

For two years (2012–2014), the Nets' mascot was the BrooklyKnight, a character created by Marvel Comics.

Up by seven points with 8:48 on the clock, the chance for an upset looked good. But Bryant led the Lakers to a 106–103 victory. Game 4 went to the Lakers, leaving the Nets without a single win.

The next year, the Nets were back. This time, they faced the San Antonio Spurs in the Finals. The Spurs clobbered them in Game 1, winning 101–89.

But the Nets were not going down without a fight. In the fourth quarter of Game 2, they were up by 11 points. Suddenly, the Spurs rallied, turning the game into a nail-biter. The Nets won by two points. The Nets ended up losing the title in six games. But their impressive Game 2 showed how they had earned their place in the Finals.

Jefferson (*left*) pushes past a defender in a 2003 Finals game.

Kidd (*center*) rushes to the basket in 2001.

NET SUPERSTARS

Any conversation about great Nets players has to begin with Julius Erving. He had a big impact on both the Nets and the game of basketball.

Nicknamed Dr. J., Erving was known for his graceful spins and forceful slam dunks. Just as exciting were his one-handed shots and passes. Erving led the Nets to two ABA Championships. He won the league's Most Valuable Player award all three years he played for the Nets.

Dr. J (*center*) scored more than 30,000 points during his 16-season career.

In their first five years in the NBA, the Nets had losing seasons. But everything turned around when the team drafted power forward Buck Williams in 1981. Reliable and hardworking, Williams was an expert rebounder and solid shooter. He won the Rookie of the Year award. In 1982, he became the first Nets player selected for the NBA All-Star Game.

Jason Kidd was another amazing Nets player. He was one of the most talented point guards ever to play in the NBA. Kidd's points, rebounds, and assists per game often ran into the double digits. At the end of his career, Kidd had the third most triple-doubles of all time.

Williams grabbed 7,576 rebounds in his eight seasons with the Nets.

NETS FACT

When Jason Collins signed with the Nets in February 2014, he became the first openly gay player in the NBA.

Collins boxes out a defender in 2014.

The year 2019 was big for the Nets. Kyrie Irving signed with the team. Irving had been Rookie of the Year in 2012. With only 53 seconds left on the clock, he scored the three-point basket that won the championship for the Cleveland Cavaliers in 2016. During his first game with the Nets, Irving set a record. He scored 50 points—the highest number of any NBA player's team debut. Off the court, Irving is known for playing a character called Uncle Drew. Uncle Drew is an older basketball player, and he has appeared in soda commercials and a 2018 movie.

Irving (*right*) sets up a shot in 2022.

Irving did not come to the Nets alone. After talking about the team with Irving, Kevin Durant also decided to sign with the Nets in 2019. Durant was already a legend who had led the Golden State Warriors to two NBA Championships. Standing almost 7 feet (2.1 m) tall, Durant has an outsized talent and sense of confidence. He is an extremely accurate shooter, able to pull off 30-foot (9.1 m) shots with ease. Heading into the 2021–2022 season, *Sports Illustrated* declared Durant the best player in the NBA.

Durant dribbles down the court in 2022.

Cam Thomas is leading the Nets into a new era.

A NEW ERA

Kevin Durant and Kyrie Irving helped make the Nets a powerhouse. But when the team signed shooting guard James Harden in 2021, the Nets looked like an unstoppable superteam.

They got off to a rough start. Durant, Irving, and Harden were all injured during the 2020–2021 season. All three stars were rarely on the court at the same time.

Many fans think Harden (*left*) is one of the best shooting guards in the NBA.

The next season was not much better. In January 2022, Durant injured his knee and missed many games. Then, the team faced another threat to their success. Irving refused to be vaccinated for COVID-19. Because of New York City's vaccination mandates, Irving couldn't play home games. After New York's mayor exempted the city's sports teams from the mandates, Irving became eligible to play at home in late March.

With Durant and Irving missing many games, the team was in danger of missing the playoffs. They decided to shake things up by trading Harden to the Philadelphia 76ers. The Brooklyn superteam had lasted only 13 months.

But die-hard Nets fans still hold out hope. With Durant, Irving, and other strong players, they are sure that very soon, their dream of a Nets NBA Championship will finally come true.

Fans were excited when Patty Mills (*center*) joined the Nets in 2021.

Bruce Brown is determined to win the NBA Championship for Nets fans.

Shawn Bradley was an aggressive player who blocked 250 shots during the 1995–1996 season.

NETS SEASON RECORD HOLDERS

POINTS

1. Rick Barry, 2,518 (1971–1972)
2. Julius Erving, 2,462 (1975–1976)
3. Julius Erving, 2,343 (1974–1975)
4. Julius Erving, 2,299 (1973–1974)
5. Vince Carter, 2,070 (2006–2007)

ASSISTS

1. Jason Kidd, 808 (2001–2002)
2. Kevin Porter, 801 (1977–1978)
3. Kenny Anderson, 784 (1993–1994)
4. Jason Kidd, 736 (2002–2003)
5. Jason Kidd, 711 (2002–2003)

REBOUNDS

1. Billy Paultz, 1,035 (1971–1972)
2. Buck Williams, 1,027 (1982–1983)
3. Buck Williams, 1,023 (1986–1987)
4. Billy Paultz, 1,015 (1972–1973)
5. Buck Williams, 1,005 (1981–1982)
   Buck Williams, 1,005 (1984–1985)

BLOCKED SHOTS

1. George Johnson, 274 (1977–1978)
2. George Johnson, 258 (1979–1980)
3. George Johnson, 253 (1978–1979)
4. Shawn Bradley, 250 (1995–1996)
5. Billy Paultz, 214 (1972–1973)

STEALS

1. Micheal Ray Richardson, 243 (1984–1985)
2. Eddie Jordan, 223 (1979–1980)
3. Brian Taylor, 221 (1974–1975)
4. Julius Erving, 207 (1975–1976)
5. Eddie Jordan, 201 (1978–1979)

THREE-POINT BASKETS

1. D'Angelo Russell, 234 (2018–2019)
2. Patty Mills, 212 (2021–2022)
3. Joe Harris, 211 (2020–2021)
4. Allen Crabbe, 201 (2017–2018)
5. Joe Harris, 183 (2018–2019)

** Stats are accurate through March 22, 2022.*

GLOSSARY

debut: first appearance

jumper: a shot made while jumping; a jump shot

overtime: an extra period of play to determine the winner of a tied game

playoffs: a series of games to determine the champion of a sports league or division

rival: a person or group that competes with and tries to defeat another

semifinal: a game or series of games coming before the final round in a tournament

slam dunk: a shot in basketball made by jumping high into the air and throwing the ball down through the basket

triple-double: the act of scoring double digits in three of five stats (assists, blocks, points, rebounds, and steals) during a single game

LEARN MORE

Brooklyn Nets
https://www.nba.com/nets/

Levit, Joe. *Meet Kevin Durant*. Minneapolis: Lerner Publications, 2023.

Monson, James. *Behind the Scenes Basketball*. Minneapolis: Lerner Publications, 2020.

NetsDaily
https://www.netsdaily.com/

Sports Illustrated Kids: Basketball
https://www.sikids.com/basketball

Wetzel, Dan. *Kevin Durant*. New York: Henry Holt, 2020.

INDEX

PHOTO ACKNOWLEDGMENTS

Image credits: Sarah Stier/Staff/Getty Images, p.4; Elsa/Staff/Getty Images, p.6; Elsa/Staff/Getty Images, p.7; Ai Wire Photo Service/Newscom, p.8; Richard Drew/AP Photo, p.9; JonP125/Wikimedia, p.10; ZappaOMati/Wikimedia, p.11; Ezra Shaw/Staff/Getty Images, p.12; Maddie Meyer/Staff/Getty Images, p.13; Ezra Shaw/Staff/Getty Images, p.14; Halvorsen brian/Wikimedia, p.15; Ezra Shaw/Staff/Getty Images, p.16; Ezra Shaw/Staff/Getty Images, p.17; Al Bello/Staff/Getty Images, p.18; Harry Harris/AP Photo, p.19; Rick Stewart/Stringer/Getty Images, p.20; Justin Edmonds/Stringer/Getty Images, p.21; Al Bello/Staff/Getty Images, p.22; Sarah Stier/Staff/Getty Images, p.23; Al Bello/Staff/Getty Images, 24; Gregory Shamus/Staff/Getty Images, p.25; Ethan Miller/Staff/Getty Images, p.26; Ethan Miller/Staff/Getty Images, p.27; TMB/Icon SMI/Getty Images, p.28

Design element: Master3D/Shutterstock.com.

Cover image: Andy Lyons/Staff/Getty Images